SPACE

Exploring Space

Robin Birch

CHELSEA
CLUBHOUSE

An Imprint of Chelsea House Publishers
A Haights Cross Communications ✦ Company
Philadelphia

This edition first published in 2003 in the United States of America by Chelsea Clubhouse, a division of Chelsea House Publishers and a subsidiary of Haights Cross Communications.

Chelsea Clubhouse
1974 Sproul Road, Suite 400
Broomall, PA 19008-0914

The Chelsea House world wide web address is www.chelseahouse.com

Library of Congress Cataloging-in-Publication Data
Birch, Robin.
  Exploring space / by Robin Birch.
   p. cm. — (Space)
  Includes index.
  ISBN 0-7910-6974-5 13.95
  1. Astronautics—Juvenile literature. 2. Outer Space—Exploration—Juvenile literature. I. Title. II. Series.
TL793 .B52 2003

2002000041

First published in 2001 by
MACMILLAN EDUCATION AUSTRALIA PTY LTD
627 Chapel Street, South Yarra, Australia, 3141

Edited by Carmel Heron and Louisa Kost
Cover and text design by Anne Stanhope

Printed in China

Acknowledgements
Cover photograph: Astronaut in Lunar Rover on the moon, courtesy of NASA, supplied by Astrovisuals.

Photographs courtesy of: AAP/Associated Press NASA TV, p. 21; AAP/Associated Press TASS-MOS TASS, p. 6; Bureau of Meteorology, p. 28; Digital Vision, pp. 5, 8, 9, 22, 26; Getty Images, p. 7; NASA, pp. 11, 12, 13, 14, 20, 25; NASA, supplied by Astrovisuals, pp. 1, 18, 19, 24, 29; NASA/Lyndon Johnson Space Center, p. 10; Photodisc, pp. 4, 17, 27; Photolibrary.com/Julian Baum/SPL, p. 23; Photolibrary.com/NASA/SPL, pp. 15, 16.

While every care has been taken to trace and acknowledge copyright the publisher tenders their apologies for any accidental infringement where copyright has proved untraceable.

Contents

Space

Space is the region beyond Earth's **atmosphere**. There is no air in space.

Spacecraft

Spacecraft are vehicles that travel through space. Some spacecraft carry people and some do not. A journey through space is called a mission.

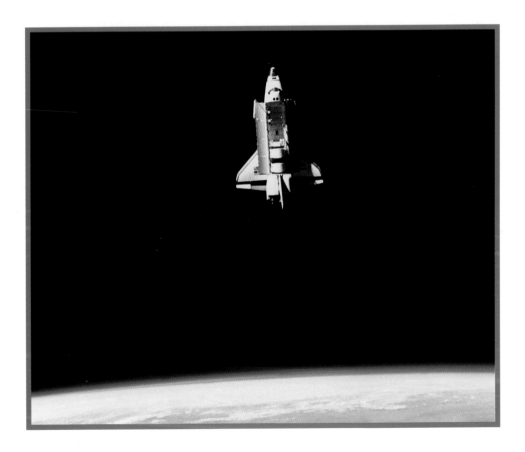

The First Spacecraft

The first spacecraft was called *Sputnik*. This metal ball was the size of a basketball. It **orbited** Earth in 1957.

The First Person in Space

Yuri Gagarin from the Soviet Union was the first person to travel in space. His spacecraft was a small **capsule** called *Vostok 1*. His 1961 journey lasted less than two hours. A person who travels in space is called an astronaut.

Space Shuttles

Today, space shuttles carry astronauts into space. Space shuttles look like airplanes. They can be used again and again. Space shuttles travel for a few weeks at a time. They orbit Earth many times. Astronauts may do science experiments or launch **satellites** during a mission.

The space shuttle take-off is called a launch. Powerful **rockets** attached to the shuttle lift it off the ground. The rockets drop off and land in the sea shortly after the launch. The shuttle then travels on its own in space. It lands back on Earth the same way an airplane does.

Astronauts in Space

People and objects are weightless in space.
Astronauts float inside the space shuttle.
They must strap themselves to the shuttle
walls to stay in one place.

Space Walks

Sometimes astronauts have jobs to do outside the space shuttle. Astronauts wear special equipment for these space walks. They put on a white space suit that has a **helmet** and its own supply of air.

Space Food

Astronauts eat sticky foods in space. Pieces of crumbly foods would float around inside the space shuttle. Some food comes dried in plastic bags. Astronauts mix in water before they eat it. They suck drinks through straws.

Space Sleep

Most astronauts float while they sleep. They might wear straps to keep from bouncing into the space shuttle's walls. Some astronauts zip themselves into sleeping bags on a wall. Straps hold them onto a soft surface and a pillow. Some astronauts wear blindfolds to block out sunlight as they sleep.

Some astronauts sleep in bags attached to a wall.

The First Moon Landing

Astronauts landed on the Moon for the first time in 1969. Their mission was called Apollo 11. Three U.S. astronauts went to the Moon in a command and service **module** called *Columbia*.

A huge rocket launched *Columbia* into space.
The rocket dropped off after the launch.

The Lunar Module

In space, two of the astronauts climbed into the lunar module called the *Eagle*. This section was joined to *Columbia*. The *Eagle* traveled to the Moon's surface. The third astronaut flew *Columbia* around the Moon while the other astronauts worked on the surface.

The two astronauts on the Moon walked on the surface. They collected rock samples to take back to Earth. People on Earth watched the astronauts on TV. The astronauts took off in the *Eagle*. They left the *Eagle's* legs on the Moon. Then they joined up with *Columbia*.

Return to Earth

The two astronauts climbed back into *Columbia*. They let the *Eagle* float away into space and headed back to Earth. Close to Earth, the astronauts separated *Columbia* into two parts. They left the service module in space. The astronauts splashed down in the ocean in the small command module.

Lunar Rovers

Astronauts made other missions to the Moon. They brought moon buggies called lunar rovers. They looked like go-carts and ran on batteries. Lunar modules carried the lunar rovers to the Moon. Astronauts left the lunar rovers there when they returned to Earth.

The International Space Station

More than 15 countries are working together to build the International Space Station. U.S. space shuttles and Russian rockets bring up the parts to build the space station. They carry one piece at a time.

The International Space Station will stay in space for many years. Crews will live and work in it for weeks or months at a time. They will travel to and from the International Space Station on space shuttles or rockets.

These astronauts are working inside a space station.

Space Probes

A space probe is a spacecraft that does not carry people. It explores space and sends photographs and information back to Earth. Some space probes bring samples back to Earth.

Voyager 1 and *Voyager 2*

The space probes *Voyager 1* and *Voyager 2* have explored the **planets** Jupiter, Saturn, Uranus, and Neptune. They took photographs that have helped scientists discover moons around these planets. The Voyager probes will explore space for many years.

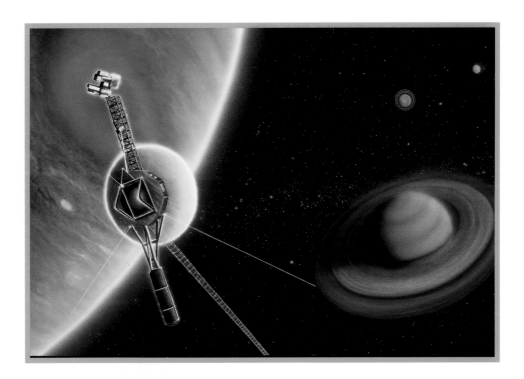

Viking 1 and *Viking 2*

The space probes *Viking 1* and *Viking 2* were sent to the planet Mars in 1975. They landed on Mars and sent photographs back to Earth. The pictures show us the surface of Mars.

Galileo

The space probe *Galileo* was launched in 1989. It arrived at Jupiter in 1995 and has been exploring the planet and its moons. *Galileo* has helped scientists make many discoveries about Jupiter's clouds and moons.

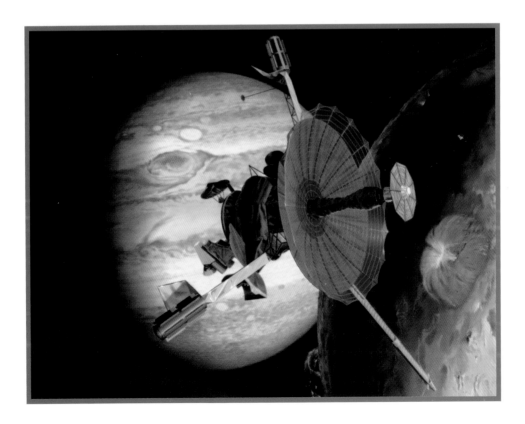

Satellites

Satellites are spacecraft that orbit Earth. They do not carry people. There are hundreds of satellites traveling around Earth.

Communications Satellites

Communications satellites send messages to TVs or telephones. The satellites receive messages from one part of Earth and send them to another part of the planet.

Observation Satellites

Observation satellites take photographs from space. People use satellite photographs of Earth to make maps. They also can learn about Earth's land, water, and weather.

This satellite photograph shows land and oceans on Earth.

The Hubble Space Telescope is a satellite that takes photographs of space. It has helped people make many new discoveries about **stars** and planets.

Space Mission Facts

Some important space missions have used space probes.

Name of Mission	Destination
Cassini	Saturn
Galileo	Jupiter
Giotto	Halley's Comet
Magellan	Venus
Mariner	Mercury
Viking 1 and 2	Mars
Voyager 1 and 2	Jupiter, Saturn, Uranus, and Neptune

Missions to the Moon were called Apollo missions. Astronauts walked on the Moon during six of the Apollo missions.

Name of Mission	Year
Apollo 11	1969
Apollo 12	1969
Apollo 14	1971
Apollo 15	1971
Apollo 16	1972
Apollo 17	1972

Glossary

atmosphere   the mixture of gases that surround a planet

capsule   a closed container

helmet   a strong head covering

module   a section of a spacecraft

orbit   to travel around an object; many spacecraft and satellites orbit Earth.

planet   a huge ball of rock or gas in space; nine planets orbit the Sun in our solar system.

rocket   a spacecraft shaped like a long tube with a pointed end; explosives launch rockets; they travel very fast.

satellite   an object that orbits a planet; many satellites made by people orbit Earth.

star   a large, burning ball of gas in space; a star gives off light and heat.

Index